Kintsugi

Poetry & Prose

Jamie Maxwell

Illustrations by:
Ai Mi Tran

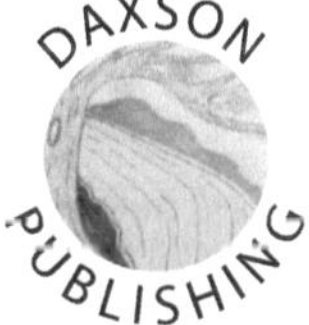

Praise for Kintsugi

"Jamie Maxwell faces reality head-on without compromising her voice. With honesty and conviction, she writes as a witness to her own truth and the world's. Kintsugi is an invitation to recognize your missing pieces—and through her words, discover the strength that binds them back together."

—Melineh Ani Yemenidjian,
The Split Pomegranate

"These poems do not simply tell a story—they carry you through it. Every verse feels like a step toward healing, toward light. Jamie Maxwell is a voice we didn't know we were waiting for."

— Ai Mi Tran, Visual Artist & Illustrator of *Kintsugi*

Kintsugi

ISBN: 9781966337263

First Edition, 2025

Printed in the United States of America

Edited by Jamie Maxwell
Cover Design by Julianne H
Layout Design by Lauren Belcher
Illustrated by Ai Mi Tran

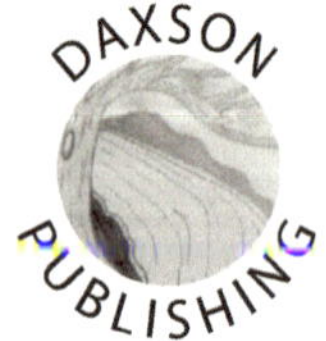

This book is dedicated to anyone who has ever been system-impacted.

Who has faced the struggle of rejection, addiction, displacement, homelessness, self-unapproval, or incarceration.

To anyone who chose resilience over the struggle.

To anyone who was ever broken and found the value in themselves.

This book is for:

> *My son Sage, who embodies his name and continues to be my wisdom.*
>
> *My sister Donna, who inspires me to be my authentic self—unapologetically.*
>
> *My Grandmother Yvonne O. Johnson, who saw and nurtured my creativity.*
>
> *My mother, who embodies the principle of kintsugi on a daily basis.*
>
> *My best friend and muse, Ai Mi Tran, for her beautiful interpretation of my poems through illustration.*

Our scars are not shameful—they are proof that we survived.

— Jamie Maxwell

"Love is an action, never simply a feeling."

— bell hooks

Kintsugi

Kintsugi Table of Contents

Foreword

by
Dr. Annahita

Mahdavi-West- Author of Dusty Relics.

I remember the first day, a few years ago, when I saw Jamie Maxwell in my class. She was a little uncertain, mostly about her own reflections. But what I saw was a beautiful, elegant Black woman with so much wisdom and strength hidden inside her. That was the beginning of her extraordinary journey in college.

She not only excelled academically but also socially and personally. The flame inside her grew so captivating, the seeds inside her so cultivating, and the love inside her so contagious. Soon she was in a leadership role mentoring and supporting her peers. I remember our conversations in my office over a hot cup of tea. Her humility was one of her shining characteristics. She was finding out who she is, at her core, a talented, brilliant, and beautiful human being. She has become what she has always been, as she tells us in her metamorphic poetry, "Conscious decisions, with each passing day, to become what I've been…"

In this deep collection of her poetry – *KINTSUGI* - Jamie Maxwell tells us the story of passing "Barriers," breaking free from the "cocoon" to wholeness, put together with golden scars that Shine the light she always had within. Her journey has taken a divine flow, and what a blessing it is to witness her glow!

Preface

The Japanese art of Kintsugi is the practice of repairing broken pottery with gold. This practice tells us something sacred: that which has been broken can become more beautiful in its mending.

When I first learned about Kintsugi, I wept. I wept for all the parts of me I once saw as broken. I thought of the traumas, the addiction, the displacement, the rejections, the systems that tried to erase me. I thought of how I had to glue myself back together, not with shame, but with gold—self-love, motherhood, recovery, purpose, and art.

This book is the gold.
These poems are the cracks filled in.

Kintsugi is for anyone who has ever believed they were too far gone.

It's a reminder that we are never broken beyond repair.
We are sacred vessels, and we are worth every drop of gold it takes to come back to ourselves.

— **Jamie Maxwell**

Notes from the Muse by Ai Mi Tran

When Jamie asked me to illustrate Kintsugi, *I didn't just say yes—I felt called. Her poems were more than words; they were portraits. In every single line, I saw the cracks that made her stronger, the softness beneath her strength, the rage that came with healing, and the joy that followed peace. This is a true testament to her character. Translating her poetry visually felt like collaborating with her inner child, her mother-self, and her warrior spirit all at once. These illustrations are not just art. They are translations of emotion, rooted in truth. Thank you, Jamie, for letting me walk beside your words with my brush.*

Kintsugi

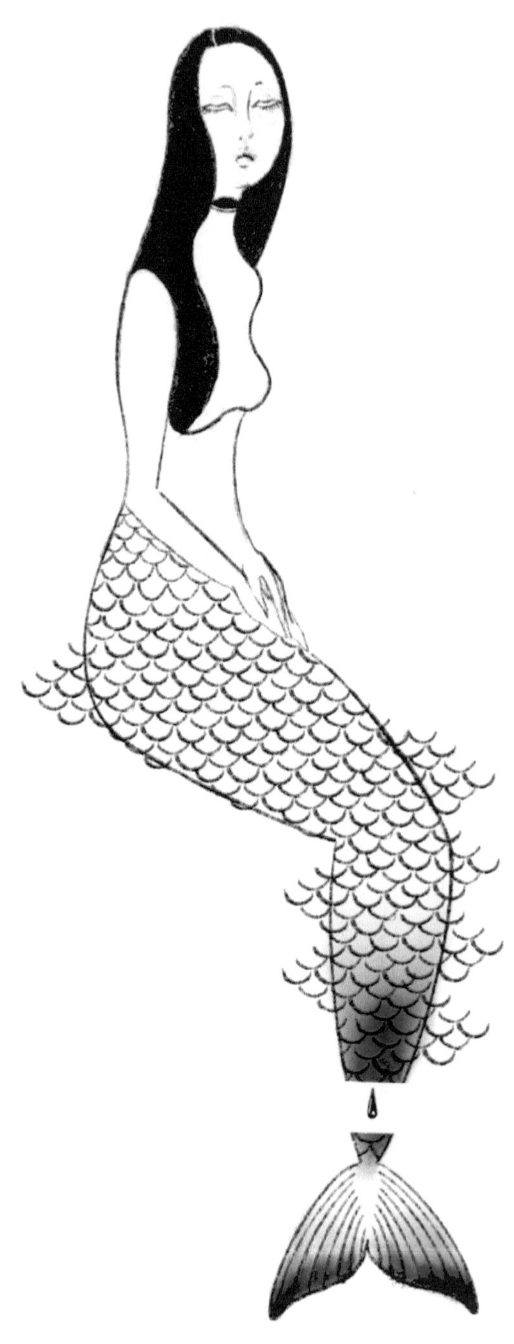

Metempsychosis

me·tem·psy·cho·sis
/ˌmedəmˌsīˈkōsəs,məˌtemsəˈkōsəs/

noun:
The supposed transmiration at death of the soul of a human being or animal into a new body of the same or different species. -
Oxford Languages

The deliberate perishing was prolonged with intention.
Existence lingering between realms, and multiple dimensions.
For she had not the strength, will, or motivation to choose life,
She had not the purpose, cause, grit, or conviction to even fight.
Burdened by the occurrences way before her own conception.
Pontificating joy, taking solace in failures she labeled lessons.
She was a seeker of many things, inquisitive by mere nature.
A keeper of unspoken dreams, still hoping for something greater.
Drawn into dark corners investigating if any light dwelled there.
The giving away of sacred self, left destitute,

broken, and bare.

She sent unanswered prayers to an unknown and silent God.
Shouldered the weight of judging stares upon her emaciated body
Beautiful masks were constructed using sins as raw material.
Upon display at night in hopes it'd be the one selected for her burial.
By poisoning and an altering of consciousness, she had to go.
Her own mind revealed the sad truths she didn't care to know.
Deteriorating further with the passing of forgotten moments and days.
Source reached out to grab hold of her, deeming her worthy to be saved.
She's as sick as her darkest secret, charted as her diagnoses.
She submitted to the idea of undergoing metempsychosis.

Barrier

Don't dare cross the line that defines my boundaries.
Eliminating any hopes of you getting close to me.
Fortified wall standing tall to protect me from the pain.
Numerous attempts have failed, yet stubbornness prevails,
Leaving the lonely with nothing else to gain.
Question myself and ask, when i'll fulfill the task,
Break down my barrier and let you in.
Such a complicated affair in trusting a friend.
Living in the shadows of disappointment, my guard stands still.
Internal dialogue questions if your intentions are real,
Two-sided thoughts leave me burdened to wonder,
As I see the frustration of access denied.
But what am i to do, i want to trust you,
But I'm too fragile and I'm protecting my pride.
Slowly I see change is a must.
An ignited flicker of trust.
My loneliness will not consume me for eternity.
Perhaps the problem truly lies in my heart of troubled lies.
For I had to learn to first fully trust me.

Big Bad Government

Big bad government may I have your undivided attention?
There's just a couple things that I would like to mention.
I understand that I'm just a mere spec on the face of this earth.
But I bear witness to the nation's abuse since birth.
Could you ever stand to get off your podium on Capitol Hill?
Step down and truly observe for my people what's always been real?
In my short-lived journey of life I've seen your kind come through here before,
making promises of a better living and fucking the people up more.
Suppressing the poor.
I could have sworn that the government was down for the people.
So why this constant impression of my people?
The Constitution states that all men are created equal.
But the history bears truth to a reality that's lethal.
I'm sick of the shit about being politically correct,
when the people keep getting screwed and the government's erect.
I just feel the need as a young seed of this nation,
to interject and expose the threats of not being

young, rich, prissed and Caucasian.
And no I don't have a racist a bias or a bitter mentality.
I just chose to expose myself to the bitter realities.
Like how the quality for lower class is constantly overlooked.
How my public school classes remain constantly overbooked.
With overused books and underpaid teachers.
A generation that took to the streets filled with false prophets and preachers.
These Divine systems of government that are supposed to servc
and protect choose to disrespect and neglect.
Hand the silver platter to those with already a couple to store upon display.
It's like we're getting hung like in the olden days.
The ways of the government are trashed away, we're trashed and slain.
Revealing them the predator and the people the prey.
Speech after speech promising new days, and new ways.
Then we see little to no progression that's our government oppression.
They say I'm less than due to the color of my skin, origin of my kin, and uncommitted sins.
Then again, I fully intend to be neglected and rejected by
a system of government only claiming to serve and protect.

That's why we keep getting screwed and the government's erect.
Big bad government can hear a plea not just coming from a woman,
once a little girl, born a minority. Who would flip through her textbooks with numerous pages missing and then try to pass the chapter test by just guessing.
Big bad government cuz you stand and get off your podium on Capitol Hill.
Step down and truly observe for my people what's always been real?

Church

I no longer feel the need to rationalize
 or justify to anyone, anything, any being, any
 entity.
I don't hold myself accountable to the masses
 of architectural construction.
Superior ideology, mind abduction.
Saints sanctifying hypocrisy,
the "self-loathing" destruction

I find it to be a congregated community
 of a mass misdirection.
Mirroring the letter of the law
 in hopes to exude perfection.
Young mind, confined, getting screwed
 by the church's erection.
The detection of demons sitting in the pulpit.

Deception, lies, embedded fear
rids me now.
Not living for life after death,
 but living for the now.
My smiles still come with the determination
 to refuse to cower.
Not live this dream in fear
 of higher powers.
Fear that when I'm dead I'll be showered
 with fire and brimstone.

Or believe without their salvation
my soul will aimlessly roam.
I've known the fate of
"salvation" based submersion.
Was oblivious to a far too obvious diversion.

The absurdity when the epitome
of reality captivates your soul!
You realize your whole life was lived
based solely on what you've been told.
These stories old, mold the structure of your core,
your mind, your inner existence
Probably why you feel this
inner resistance

So, No….
No I will never apologize or repent
For my biological, chemical, spiritual makeup
Or allow myself to be engulfed
by this refusal to "WAKE UP"
Open eyes to lies passed down like heirlooms
or traditions.
Petitioning souls offering external redemption.

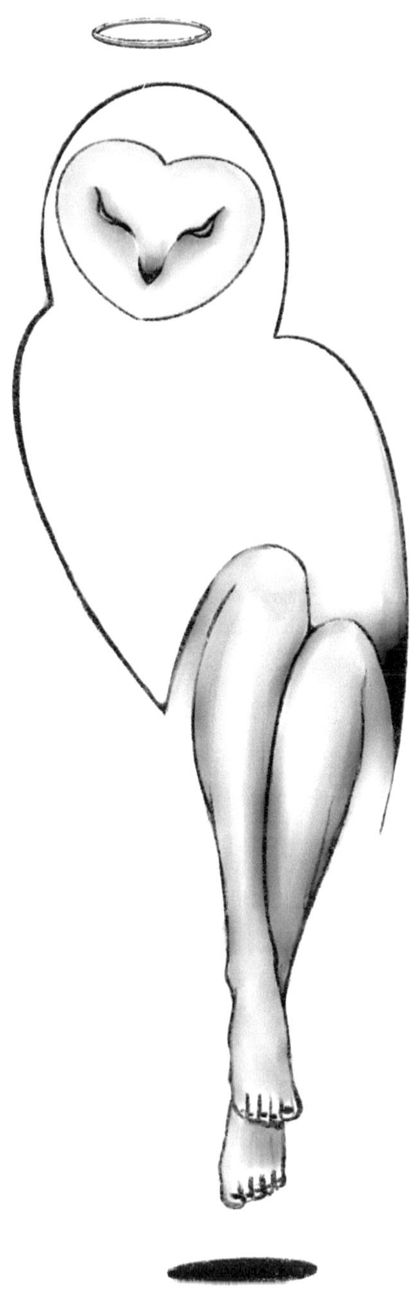

Conscious Evolution

I'm striving to evolve,
a desperate need,
some claim it's nature,
a course to heed.
Human experience,
vast and free,
yet for me, a choice,
a constant decree.

Conscious decisions,
with each passing day,
to become what I've been,
in a different way.
Adapting, morphing,
traits anew,
daily commitment,
a path to pursue.

In the mirror's reflection,
a new image takes hold,
conscious evolution,
a story unfolds.

Consequential Love

And then he asked me....
What my definition of love consisted of...

My response was that I didn't know,
I had never really thought about it.
So I really got to thinking about it.
I realized that the first time I was introduced to the concept of the word love, my initial response to its existence was confusion.
Love equated to contradiction.
Love was an intransitive verb not a noun..
Love should've been a definitive, declaration statement.
I love you!
But oftentimes I found it to be a word accompanied by other words.
Words like but.
Granny always said Mama loved my sister and I,
But Mama couldn't help the fact that she couldn't raise us.
Papa always said he really loved Granny,
But he hit her sometimes.
Once so hard it shattered her ear drum.
Now we always gotta lean in real close.
"I can't hear you baby, speak into my good ear," she'd say.

So the first time a man raised his hand to me, I heard the message loud and clear. He loved me
But I just made him so angry.

His love usually found the company alongside other words like "if"
If I really loved him I would *fill in the blank*
Love should have been a force that could be identified by actions not accompanying adverbs.
How could I allow my response to be that my definition of love consisted of fragmented sentences.
Subject with no predicate.
Avoiding the subject, I was a victim of predators, and how the predicate of that sentence made it predictable.
Love could be spotted with a face that resembled that of a consequence.
I responded, "Love is consequential."

Directions to Friendship

My overwhelming desire is to simply acquire the directions to your friendship.
Perhaps manifest bonds, far more intimate than kinship.
I've been spent endless energy investigating the equation of who you truly .
Hoping, I might see a reflection of self, when emerging into your lively seas.
I wish to learn to read you like a page-marked book.
Allowing me to decode the mystery behind your penetrating looks.
For you have taken all curiosity I currently possess, have left….
Making me want to be one of the ones who brings out your best.
I have yet to contest that I am invested in you.
Somewhat highly impressed by you.
Harvesting a new feeling of being I never really had to attest to.
Permit me to grab hold of your soul.
Let us embark on the greatest story never told.
Like when it rains, I'll lay my head on your chest and let the rhythmic beats alone speak of your heart's distress.
And when it pours, I'll warm your innermost core,
Mend your broken wings, so that you're able to

soar.
It'll never matter how the seasons change.
All that'll ever matter is that our friendship remains.
My overwhelming desire is to simply acquire directions to your friendship.
Manifesting bonds far more intimate than kinship.

First Love / Drug

I promised myself in the bliss of being wanted that
I wouldn't forget.
Allow the memories of internal ecstasy wrapped
up in this vibrant,
neat, dark chocolate package to ever be erased.
Now that he's left my heart I find traces of him,
between there and my mind,
His remains I find trapped in my throat and I can't
swallow.
Perhaps that's why his name still lingers there,
often escaping my lips with this reminiscent air.
So though indifference is constant I still find
myself haunted,
the romantic tragedy played out when I was a teen.
Or the reel, of the scene, of the feen, that possessed
my being.
When then blow called love, hit too low,
and knocked the wind out of me.
He became the first gasps of air I was breathing,
he sensed my needing for that masculine love.
potent highs ensued, then he began to wean me off
the drug.
Held high up on his pedestal, my soul was left
broken from the fall.
When I tried to leave for good, I couldn't.
I could barely crawl.
I'd look up for guidance but only his image would

appear there.
Perhaps it was the illusion of the dark-tinted shades I chose to wear.
I wrapped the singular thread he left dangling from his coattails around my wrist,
For the hope of experiencing bliss I negated my pride.
I clung to every word he said, he insisted one day I'd be his bride.
I had illusions of grandeur, of making him my king.
I was blindsided when the delusions and slander began to consume me.
A love that constantly eludes you isn't real.
My first love was a drug,
And I had to swallow that pill.

Let Me Be Man

I can't be woman residing
in this body any longer.
The weightiness of an empty womb,
so full of potential.
The crease of my stretch marks
 showing how I can't decide rather to be
 too big, Or too small.
The folds of my belly telling the story
of how much I've given in to hunger.
Plagued by the softness of my bosom
 which all the wrong folks have made their haven.
My freshly manicured nails that scratched
out of another's head, good thoughts
they took to cash in with no credit to me.

I can't be woman residing
in this body any longer.
So let me be man.
Let me default to logic and solution,
and put emotion in its place.
Let me be man populating
wombs with my seed.
Let me be protector and provider,
and construct monuments,
that favor my endeavors.

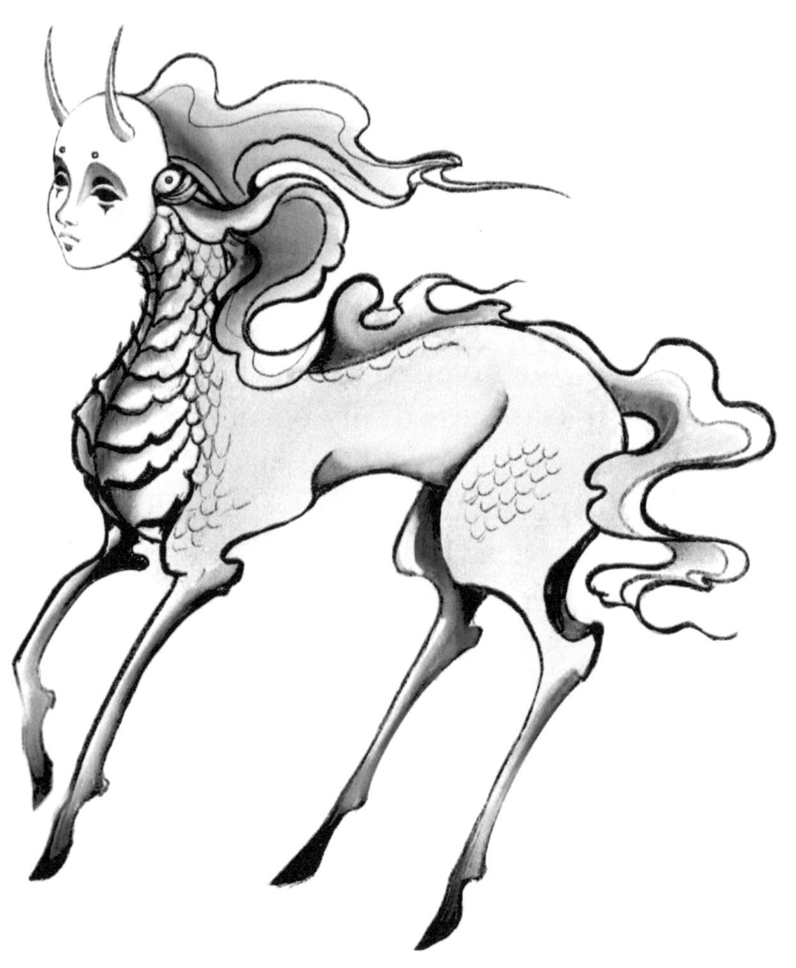

Matters

I hope this time that it matters.
Matters like when my pen splatters ink,
Meticulously, lyrically, poetic me
Dancing subjects and predicates across
the worn down pages of my composition books.
Matters like it's been so cold out that teeth chatter.
Matters like the plague of generational curses,
and how we must break the vicious pattern.
My planet Venus, mind trapped in an undiscovered
 galaxy between here and Saturn.
Could love bloom if I visit his Neptune?
I am a millennial woman, manifestation of source,
I take roads less traveled, while still staying the
course.
Woman came from Adam.
I know Adam came from Atoms.
 I wonder then does it even matter,
If my heart's given, then clumsily handled and
shatters?
Aren't we all just projections, artistic splatter?
I intend to mend the distance that this existence
defines.
A tangible love that matters could never possess
 another and label them "Mine"
I wanna defy the concept of time.
I wanna live out the narration of my rhymes.
 So won't you, make it matter this time?

Never Fall in Love

As of late I've been elated,
to rise to this grand occasion.
I'm too wise to be persuaded,
to ever fall in love again.
I've been manifesting,
burning sage, lighting candles,
conscious, and not dazed.
Not phased by those days,
when I had yet to find a friend.
I wrote a list and I insisted,
that the trajectory be shifted,
presentation of his presence,
is presently such a gift.
Intentionally he's constant,
decided not to be haunted,
by fears trauma's constructed,
now I label them a myth.
I'm enveloped in the optimism,
light shining through the prism,
Reaching out with both hands.
We boldly grab hold of it.
Each day that we persist,
we're convinced of what it is.
He'll ask me what I'm feeling,
and the sentiments endearing,
What I'm fearing eclipses the poetry,
so what I'm aiming for I miss.

the unknown can be alluring,
a sure thing is far less boring.
The adventure is knowing I am his.
I prayed, and spirit told me,
there's a blessing in the midst.
Reflective light that illuminates,
through the dark abyss.
He's got questions…
Perhaps they're how?, or what?…
The solution is to trust.
What has been answered is the why.
Any doubt dissipates for me,
landing amongst the comfort of kind eyes.
Taking orbit when he meditates,
between thighs.
We plan for a future,
draft out timelines,
daydream about sweet things,
like time traveling together.
Venturing between time zones,
sharing our adventures on our timelines.
Folks liking our status on their iphones.

Choosing gratitude together,
Neither of us has to do this life alone.
I take solace in dreams without the threat of
nightmares.
I take refuge in words of I love you,
coupled with the actions that show care.
I am present in the mere presence,
not wishing to be elsewhere.

When the standards are set so high,
I’ve no choice but to meet love there.
So I didn’t have to fall in love again.

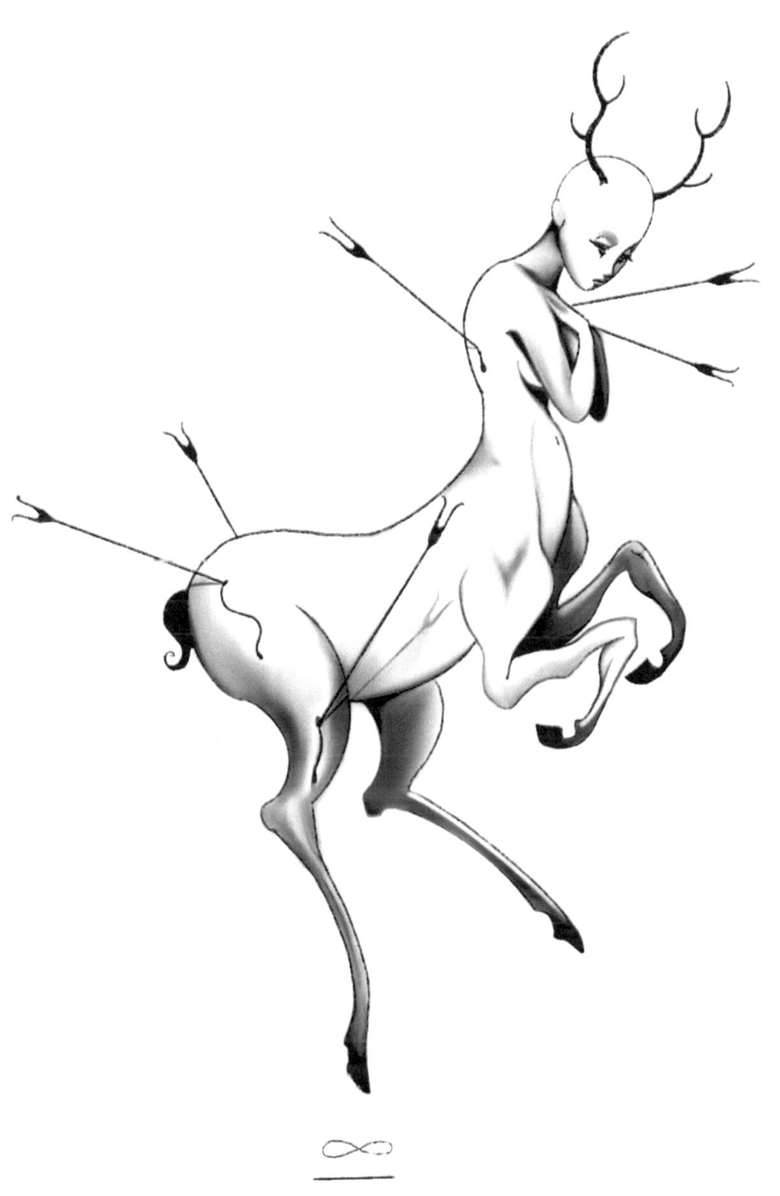

Next June

I stare at you sleeping,
I know by next June
and a full moon from now,
your face will be but
a distant memory.

As you slumber
I listen to your
shallow breathing,
inhale the scent of you.
Nestle myself into the
crevice where chest
and shoulder meet.

Once this bed is
no longer ours,
I'll return to Venus,
you'll return to Mars.
The blistering wounds,
will be faded scars,
there will be no trace,
that we ever took place.

Lose myself in our kisses,
Soon I will miss it.
It'll be a while,
until another's lips,

meet mine.
You bring me coffee,
in bed, in the morning.
Dark roast coupled
with caramel creamer.
I sip it slowly.
The bittersweetness,
embodies what we've
become.

I've been setting the
table for two,
not yet prepared,
to eat alone.
I booked, 3 solo trips,
in the next year.
Two King sized beds.
Just to prove,
to myself, or us,
there was always room,
for you.

Embraces are haunting,
your eyes reveal,
the distance between us.
Reality daunting,
I can't equate your words
as something to trust.

Between pointing fingers,
we linger in the chasm.

Loiter in indifference.
Relish in the pockets of joy.
So far, so few,
in between.
Our I love you's,
sound more like Goodbyes.

Heart space still has a
place for you.
Logical mind anticipating
the departure.
Wet face, knowing
there will be no ring
from you.
Nearing final chapters,
wishing I was the author.

Loving you feels like failing.
Wanting you feels like defeat.
Holding on, to a damp railing.
Laid up next to a stranger
I once knew, hoping
we could again meet.

I'll cling to you,
for a few more days,
or months.
I've been drained, you've
been dehydrated.
Relentlessly trying to
pour from empty cups.

Preparing ourselves,
for the inevitable break up.

No Intentions

We both affirmed that neither of us had any real intentions.

I resent that this lack of intent was ambushed by utter intrigue.

Something transformed within us.

We morphed into mathematicians, magicians and musicians.

We perched upon the edge of my bed.

Nestled ourselves away into cocoons. Meditated.

When he inhaled and exhaled,

I mimicked his breathing.

Tried to match the rhythm.

We scratched and nibbled, clawed and chewed.

Discovered ignorances about ourselves we never knew.

He exposed my hidden instrument and played

melodic tunes.

Both falsetto and baritone octaves were exhausted.

He'd ask questions about things he assumed I knew answers to.

I tried to solve algorithms.

I feared immersing myself into a book with only one chapter.

Felt the hesitancy of turning the first page with not another after.

Tirelessly avoiding yet another sad story.

How can someone so intense be so vague?

I knew this experience would be a plague.

The truth is, I just wanted to heal him.

Help him to face his wounds head on.

Dress them in hemp leaf saturated with aloe and affirmations.

Witness the fading of scars.

Only then would I reveal my own bandages.

Peel away at the dirty, tattered remains of them.

Expose him to the once festering wounds.

Now renewed flesh with fresh scarred tissue.

Ode to Lauryn, Part 1

Music has a way o captivating you,
bringing you into its loving folds.
At age 14 I heard the Lauryn Hill unplugged
album
Disc 1, song 12
Lauryn said "I gotta find my peace of mind".
All I've ever felt that this world wanted was a
piece of mine.
Even with acquired wealth, earned merit, and
unsolicited accolades
it eludes the seeker to find.
More so than my addictions, I fiend for an
unknown soothing,
an inner contentment.
Or perhaps a sense of purpose, when I was feeling
worthless.
We wander blindly in dense forest, in dim
lightning seeking refuge.
We cower in fear of the unknown.
We start off with full innocence and hope.
And then life chips away at our humanity.
We submit to the insanity.
Generational belief systems plague our existence.
I too became a victim of Institutional recruitment,
and a dependant on the general relief system,
Generally if I ever did find relief, it was brief.
Master still doles out rationings.
Fashioning field niggas to believe in the notion

that being a house nigga is a promotion
We done been drank the potion
Like grape juice accompanied by stale crackers on communion Sunday
Standing in line, questioning why our benefits are $221 a month in cash.
$187 dollars in food provided the choice, presented the task,
Either sell my flesh, sell out, or sell my soul.
Couldn't pay the toll... Couldn't live with that being my fate
Could I recreate the narrative?
Or spin the lies until they resembled a truth I could tolerate.
Or embrace that the fact I survived without all consuming self-hate is perhaps what made me great.
I had to be stronger, I had to be better
I wasn't going to any longer, take from the next man for the next dollar,
Wasn't going to hop in that Benz just because a nigga hollered.
Wasn't destined to call some pimp " Daddy" and just use the excuse that I grew up without a father.
Once upon a time I became the very stereotypes I was trying to disprove.
I lived and became a reincarnation of my family curses.
I wanted to rally the congregated community of the masses of misconception and disperse it.
I wanted to have conviction in those ideologies

that taunted me for so long,
pulsed into my veins like my genetic DNA, and
forever doomed me to the pits of hell.
Wanted to escape the impending fire and
brimstone the God I inherited warned me of.
I've survived hell before.
I've survived the man I love calling me whore.
I survived the puddles of my own vomit and
blood, and tears upon the bathroom floor.
I wanted so much to be linked to my unknown
tribe, that I sold my soul back into captivity.
I wanted so much to find a righteous theology,
that in my search I found sin and became the very
epitome…
Of the very thing I strived to never be.

Shrinking

I almost believed you when you told me I was too much.
Took inventory of my mass and sectioned off pieces of myself to cut away.
Disposed of the excess of me at open mics and in poetry books.

I wanted to sweeten my aura to make myself more palatable.
Hoped I could mask the taste of the bitterness with sweet nothings.
I wanted to be digestible to you.

Folded into myself hoping I'd shrink enough for you to decide that
I was light enough to be carried.

My feet bore the miniscule scrapes from what had become the ritual of walking on eggshells.
My blouses were saturated with my own spit from holding my tongue.
I contorted and bent backwards in an attempt to fit into the box
that you'd constructed for me.

Adapted the habit of confining my feelings to my journal,

where you told me they belonged.
Emotions wandering around freely grew repulsive to you.

So I kept them quarantined in fear they'd infect us.
My reflection began to resemble less of anyone I remembered.
My short term memory and ability to recollect was negotiated away from me.
I was charred and disfigured from all the gaslighting.

I couldn't love myself and you simultaneously.
So I choose you initially.
Hoping you'd love me enough for the both of us.

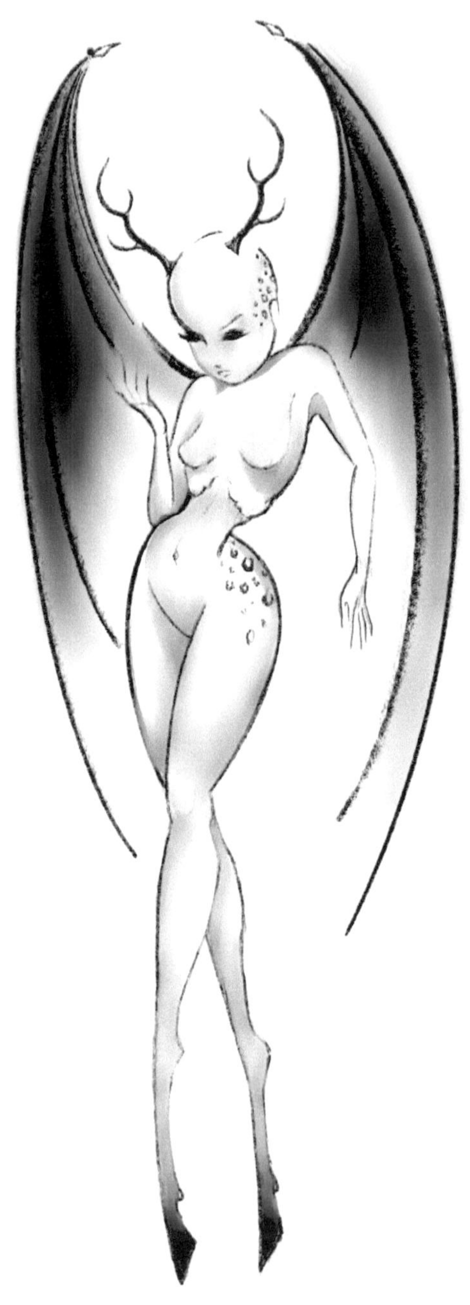

Ode to Lauryn, Part 2

Lauryn said you gotta find your peace of mind.
My chemical and spiritual makeup is only by divine design.
Why did I believe the masses when they told me I wasn't good enough?
In adolescence Granny sent me to the "good schools" with the white folk and I had no Sense of self.
They asked me why my hair curled so tight against my scalp,
Why my skin was so dark, and why my family didn't possess wealth?
An insult hurled that consumed me and affected my mental health.
That's the first time I realized, I lived in a world where I'd be excluded.
They asked me who my father was…
And that's when I became a writer and performer
Scripting and Ad libbing my version of the Cosby Show
As long as they didn't know.
Finding out the truth about my father was a fatal blow
I became good at putting on a show
The Irony that Granny wrote and produced
Christian plays with the salvation message
Yet had no salvation from her internal oppressions.

She proved to be my first real life lesson
Lauryn said you gotta find your peace of mind,
The system tends to make an example of you when you refuse to be confined.
The burden to bear at the end of the day is solely mine.
The penetrating stares have never defined me.
Perhaps my light shines too brightly, so much so that it was blinding.
My higher power is the peace that passes all understanding.
I was a bible breed, theology feed, living for their promise of heaven.
Philippians 4:7, Titus 2:11 and 12
We tend to dig and delve, further into our own self-made ditches.
The first man I ever loved was my Grandfather.
My personal hell not prophesied was littered with the terms of endearment he gave me like "dizzy broad," "trifling heifer" and "stupid bitches"
Another man I loved, I allowed him to inflict me with his drug of choice, followed by the need for stitches.
When I left the church, burnt my sage, collected crystals they labeled me a witch.
The ones you love are the first ones to call you out the name they gave you
But we live amongst more sheep than shepherds, so hard to cast blame.
First ones to reject you are those from which you came.

I’ll be bright magic and heretic.
I’ll solve perceived problems like arithmetic.
I break chains and adorn myself with the broken pieces
Shaping them into a crown
Since I gritted my teeth so long, I choose to just smile
My clenched fist now is the opening and closing of hands now, motioning folks unto me.
My broken walk from an aching back, is now the choreography of my African dance.
I got a second chance.
I bore a man child whom I can raise to be everything that his daddy wasn’t to me, and put him back into the rotation of this world to love a woman right…endlessly.
The scripture said the one who seeks will find.
Lauryn said…
I gotta…..
Find my peace of mind.

Pay for Your Own High

If I put the substances down,
finally inhaled reality,
allowed the smoke to clear,
perhaps I'd realize my true capacity
— for success?
My inner best has been suppressed,
by the self-imposed stress?
the mere lack of rest…
this constant need to detest.
Seldom am I my best,
'cuz the Kush is so compelling.
Oftentimes, my thoughts
become so overwhelming.
I'm frequently told that I'm out of control.
Thoughts expand to a mass so colossal,
That I'm able to conceal myself behind them,
Rarely do I make any
real efforts to find them,
I barely make any real efforts
to see them.
So now instead of having the habits,
I've allowed myself to be them.
If my sum is just a habit—-
And am I too used up that fast?
My inner worth got to be worth
more than a few dub sacks,
head change nestled in the bottom

of a crushed Newport pack.
Never imagined at year nineteen,
this would be the whole sum of my being.
My man's gotta be disgraced
to be calling me Queen.
Reeking with Gin,
my people have to hesitate
when calling me kin.
Burdened with sins,
I feel like God isn't even claiming me his.
I've just been wanting to feel the love,
but now I'm just claimed by the thizz'
I'm geeked up,
dead inside—
yet still claiming to live.
Even I'm disturbed by the habits,
I'm praying like "Somethings gotta give."
I've been starting to find the small
jest in life in order to survive and rise.
I'm starting to realize it's worth
finding the blessings in the disguise.
Understanding that there's no team in I.
When having an addiction,
You eventually have to pay for your own high.

**thizz - a slang term, referencing the drug ecstasy*

Plight of a King

Dear King,
Please know

Divine universe designed us to
go with the flow,
All things are working out
or the highest good,

The things we don't want to do
The most
are probably the ones
that we really should.

Like when forgiving your past be the task,
One thing constantly rings true,
it ain't really for them but more so for you.

I know you can attest to
how it feels to be defeated.
Did your best, but still left you
feeling not needed.
Giving the core of yourself,
and they giving you less.

I know you're tired from
chasing the dream,
and running out of breath.

Set out to be their peace and
they're set on causing stress.

I too have suffered the plight,
when you're looking for resolution,
and they're just looking to fight.

Come claim your throne, King,
if they ain't treating you right.

Perhaps you were told that
a good thing had grown old,
her shoulder cold,
said you were seeking too much.
The simple things became
much more complex.
Wanting words of affirmation,
or simply wanting their touch.

Or was it that nothing seemed
to be given freely anymore?
everything had to be earned.
Yearned to be close to love's flame,
You let them close and got burned.
Did they have the capacity
without catastrophe,
to step back, silence ego,
seek first wisdom that is yet to be learned?

I too have suffered the plight,
Was your critique rejected or

received with pure spite?
Come claim your throne, King,
if they ain't treating you right.

Did your last love know
the significance of service?
to show you how much you're deserving?

Were you kicked when
you were down?
Though they knew how much
you were already hurting?

Did they know the wonders of
speaking life into your existence
and affirming you with their words?
Did your request often fall on deaf ears,
leaving you feeling unheard?

It's beyond the realm of obscenities
to intentionally dethrone
your own King,
and then expecting a ring.
It's like rejecting the divinity of
a possible Kingdom.

To whoever my future King I would say,
if in the past the load's been too heavy
go on ahead and make it light.
I too have suffered the plight.
Come claim your throne, King,

if they ain't treating you right.

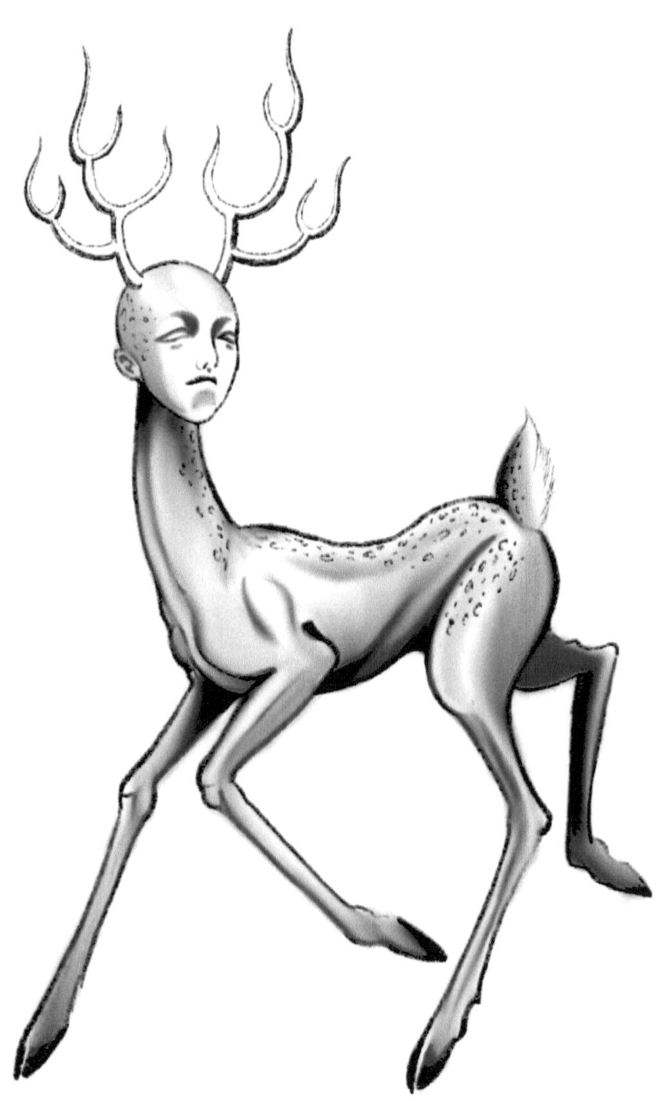

Sonshine

I can't forget that moment,
I would never want to,
So much fear, and fortitude, and awe.
For I had been chosen,
and been given purpose.

I stared at that sanctified white test,
and those bold blue lines intersecting
to reveal the crucifix,
I knew just like the Messiah,
I would sacrifice my life for you.
I watched, like an outsider looking in as my body
—changed.

morphing, belly stretching, shifting,
making room for you.
Breast swollen, and tender,
producing nutrients to nourish and sustain.
Hips widening, cervix elongating.
My temple became your cocoon and resting place.
And then came,
— your glorious arrival.

Water breaking, flowing red carpet laid out,
for the most prominent guest.
Beating heart no longer in my chest,
instead transported to wherever you are.

The most luminous and best part of me
encapsulated,
—in your form.

Full face, rounded cheeks,
warm and rich big brown eyes.
Sticky hands, loving strokes on Mama's face.
Melodic silly giggles sound like jazz symphonies.
Aromatic scents, Johnson and Johnson,
melatonin lavender upon a moist damp neck.

The peace of you nestling against me,
your demand for comfort.
Your existence is a call to action.
Your dreams became my mission.
My sonshine.

Too vibrant to stare at too long,
For fear my eyes might begin to water
And never cease.

What Cocoon Feels Like

This place is foreign yet it
offers sanctuary.
I must be a caterpillar.
This must be my cocoon.
Though my bones ache and throb,
though my body is inactive
and sedentary.

Though my breaths are short
and labored.
Though my skin is taut and tender
and transparent.
Though I am stretching beyond
limits and capacity,
though I am trying to
hold it all in.
Though I am trying to
let it all go.

Though my head throbs
with each memory.
Though I'm strained
from remembering it all.
though I've never received
the gift of forgetting.

Though my teeth are brittle,

chipped, decaying
— falling out
Though my lips cracked and split,
and silent.
Though my mouth is dry,
I'm dehydrated.
Though their kisses
have never been soothing.

Though embraces feel like
strangulation or suffocation.
Though the loneliness
feels like suffering.
Though this place is foreign
yet it offers sanctuary.

I must be a caterpillar.
This must be my cocoon

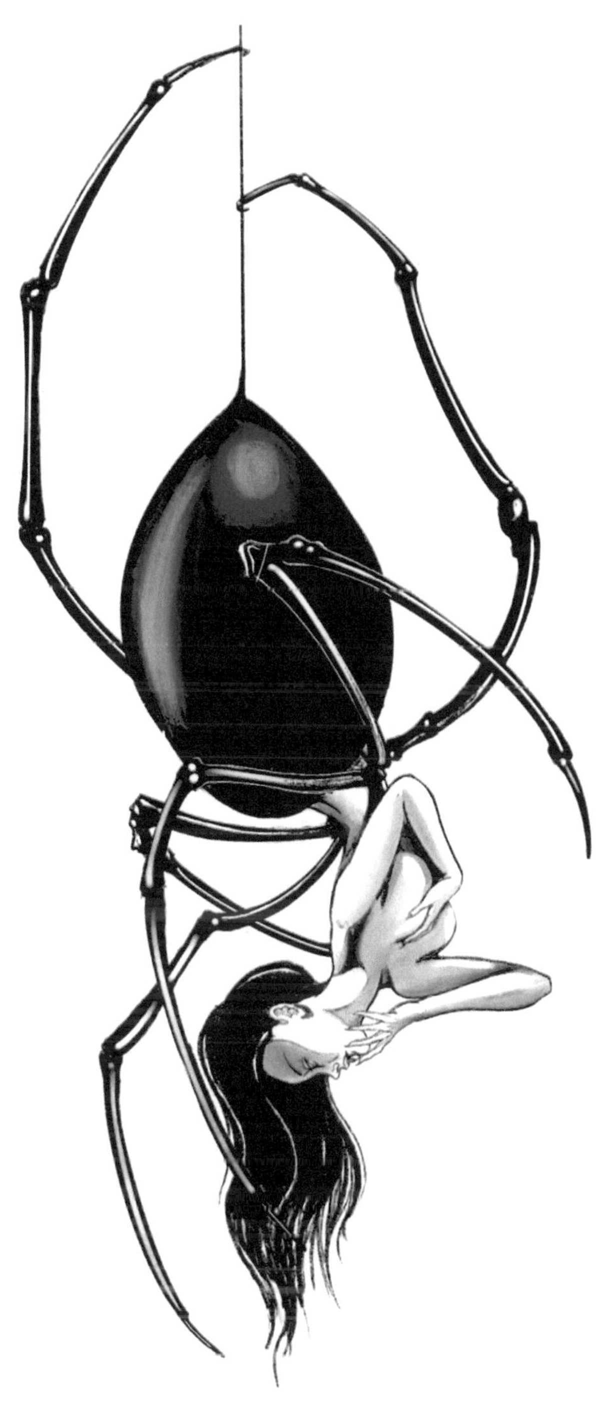

Deliverance

Deliverance from my mind I keep losing.
From the bondage of the depths of my soul,
To the inner being that makes me whole.

I felt exuberant from the fatal loins of
myself,
rescuing me,
helping me,
protecting me,

It's ironic how my mind is at war with my
soul,

And my body is making me choose
so I'm not whole.

But I will survive this battle with myself,
Not neglecting that, I started it.

And that this battle that seems I can't win,
Would drive me to an unfathomable rage
Against whom the divine had created.
To conquer my inner being.
And to receive Deliverance.

Unspoken

I promised I'd never mention it.
Nor would I ever speak it into existence.
Because once I did it, I'd be admitting something happened,
see now I'm trapped in and I can't escape the memories.
So I flee from the scene like a criminal flees.
Acts were more than criminal but the victim is me.
There. I said it. I'm a victim.
I've always hated that title so I remove the label
but the residue still sticks to me.
Just like the memories, of abuse that happened
at age three.
Or perhaps lack of recollection,
re-written, and interpreted accounts of a child no longer able to be,
Just Age Three.

So many times before a court appointed therapist,
or preacher
Social Worker,
or teacher

Would ask me…
"Jamie, How old were you when it started?"
Then I would reply,
I mean I would deny,

I mean I would straight lie,
and say I didn't remember.

Lying always seemed to be easier than telling the truth,
or acknowledging the men who I trusted
that betrayed the innocence of my youth.

At age eleven, I learned to be silent.
If violations were unspoken of, it's almost like they never happened.

Silence secures secrets,
Until whispers turn into screams.
Until nightmares replace dreams.
Until queens become feens.

Can something be taken that is already given away?
Can one still be victim, if they willingly give themselves up as prey?

At age 15, and 18, and 21.
I started to wonder.

Is my body still a temple, if it's where the devils chose to lay
Am i even worthy of redemption,

If I no longer pray?
If I'm no longer prey.

I found within myself that I'm still stronger than ever.
And what didn't kill me, only made me better.
My skin has thickened now to endure the harsh weather.
I gathered the pieces of my past, which I had chosen to sever
and allowed them to make me better.
I'm allowing it to let it make me whole.
I can't blame myself for things that were out of my control.

Although I promised I'd never mention it,
Nor would I ever speak it into existence.
The residue still sticks to me.

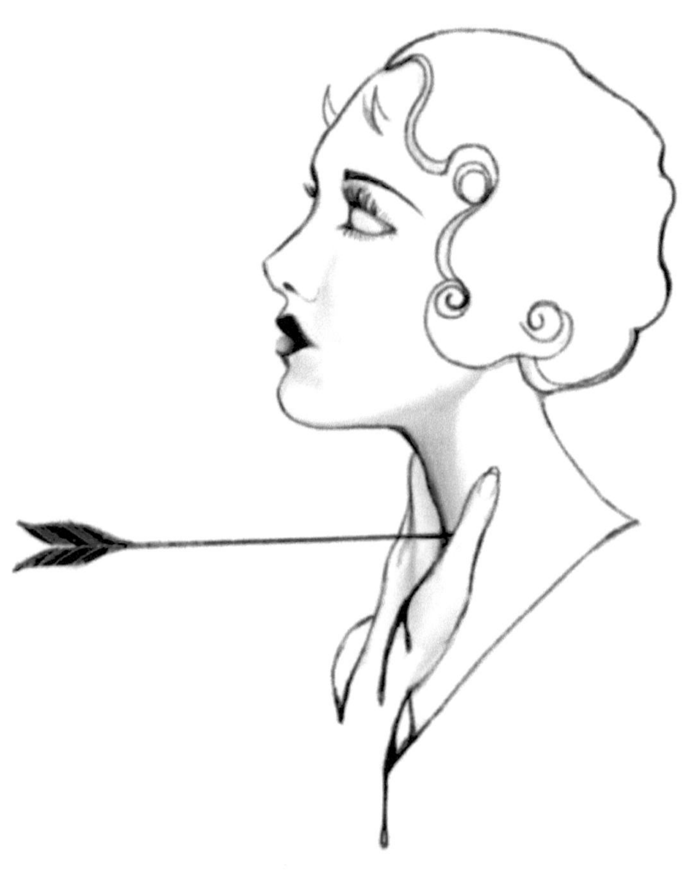

Good Soil

I am a tree hugger.
I go and search out the biggest tree
to admire,
and I want to love it.
Why does standing next to the biggest tree,
cause me to shrink?

Big trees 'posed to reach for heaven.
Big trees 'posed to caress the wings of birds.
Big trees 'posed to kiss the clouds.
Big trees 'posed to clean the air.

So why do trees leave me with no oxygen?

Tree said he wanted to plant his seed
into rich and good soil....
Good soil 'posed to provide
everything a seed needs to thrive.
Good soil 'posed to
nurture that seed into a tree.
Nourish the roots,
and support seed,
until it can stand upright.
So that's what I tried to be.

Big trees 'posed to reach for heaven.
Big trees 'posed to caress the wings of birds.

Big trees 'posed to kiss the clouds.
Big trees 'posed to clean the air.

Something foreign has taken root,
the seed blossomed,
Into wisdom
I named him Sage and now,
he will forever be my greatest love
for all of my days...
I never questioned the big tree...
Never doubted the source,
This tree swaying any way
the wind blew,
shedding leaves,
falling where they may.
Providing shelter for strays.

Big trees 'posed to reach for heaven.
Big trees 'posed to caress the wings of birds.
Big trees 'posed to kiss the clouds.
Big trees 'posed to clean the air.

I am a tree hugger.
I go and search out the biggest tree
to admire,
and I want to love it.
Why does standing next to the biggest tree,
cause me to shrink?
I'm all wrapped up round this rough,
peeling bark.
Holding on firmly,

to this inanimate matter.
Saying
"Oooh how I love these trees,
don't cut um down."
Strapping myself in chains to it,
creating cute rhyming phrases for um,
Like
"Save the trees y'all"
"Save the rainforest"
"Save them all"
Even when there's not even enough rain for us,
We dehydrated.
The trees need to reign....
When bulldozers come.
I stay firm,
For I'm good soil.

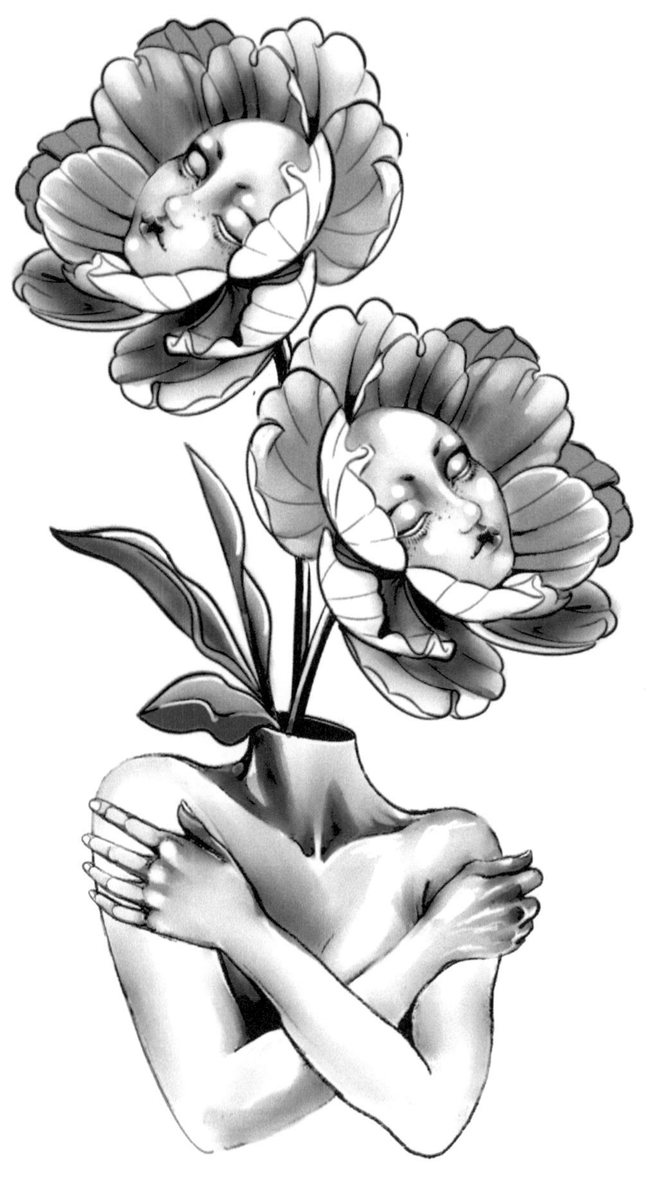

Comma.

Often used, conceptualized as pause.

Perhaps needed to add emphasis,

Or an anticipatory resolve.

Segregating Subjects from Predicates.

Relegating nouns and verbs etiquette,

Acting as barrier between what

Has already transpired,

And what is yet to come.

I'd guess being a comma is lonely.

Not sharing the importance

or the finite period, or the

excitement of an exclamation.

Usually ignored or avoided

by the declarative statement.

Lingering in the in between.

In a constant state of waiting.

I’d implore commas to take resolve,

In between the effect and cause.

To relish in the comfort that,

A comma holds significance.

It’s very existence is a call

to action. A remembrance

that the story is not yet over.

The best has yet to come.

Covert

Surviving the trauma of experiencing the covert narcissist is like
transplanting the still viable parts of a broken heart into
a mind that has gone brain dead.

It's like disarming the love bomb that is ticking within your spirit,
not knowing which wire to cut. Is it blue or is it red?

It is fearing the catastrophe of making the wrong choice.
Again.
It is an alteration of your tonality
to the point you have no voice.
It is immersing yourself into the reality
that they have trafficked you into.
It is conforming to their belief system,
abandoning the one that you once knew.
It is Stockholm syndrome personified.
It is questioning your own reality.

It is apologizing for asking for the narcissist to apologize.
it is sequestering your emotions,
your better judgement is quarantined

and the endless test you've been given
renders all false positives.

Cognitive Dissonance leaves you in a perpetual state of confusion.
You attempt to bargain with nothing left to give in return.
You are praying the removal prayer to your higher power,
and the rico sweep lives your pillow cases drenched in your weeping.
Trauma Bond reminds you how lonely, lonely can get.

Rumination leaves you replaying scenarios
the narcissist has made you question ever even existed.
Scouring through past scenarios trying to figure out how you missed it.
Mistaking red flags for a carnival full of rides with no thrills.
In the end you're left questioning if any of it was real.

The things that were once so sacred are taken.
The things you wanted the most are withheld.
The dream you thought you lived in becomes a nightmare.

I translated those initial smiles and “I love you’s”
and acts of service as my purpose.
Poisoned by potential proving not to be very
potent.
Finally finding the antidote in my own throat
once I managed to whisper the words “I love you”
to myself.

Took a thorough inventory, just to realize that
all the things I demanded from someone else.
I already possessed it.
I just needed to cry enough for my vision to
become clearer.
I just needed a soul death, to draw my creator near.

Kintsugi

Wabi-sabi

We accept what is, there is no urge to change,
In chips and dents, there's no need for exchange.
Though broken, we do not collapse or fall,
For beauty lives within us all.

In flaws and cracks, we find delight,
They turn to gold when met with light.
And we celebrate what's torn apart,
Repair reveals the truest form of art.

What once was built for our daily use,
Now bears a tale of deeper truths.
Each break, a sign of service done
Not weakness, but where strength's begun.

Mushin

No clinging to the form once known,
We bless the seeds that change has sown.
Each fracture marks a turning stage,
A chapter inked on life's old page.
We bow to time, to fate's embrace,
To cracks that give new truths a face.
In every scar, a story lies
Of loss, of growth, of healing ties.

Imperfection, grace, and history
Resilience shaped through Kintsugi.

Final Word: The Gold Is You

If you take nothing else from this book, please take this:

You are not your past. You are not your pain. You are not your failures.

You are your comeback. You are your courage. You are every single time you choose to heal instead of hide.

You are gold

—poured into your broken places.
You are the art.
You are the masterpiece.

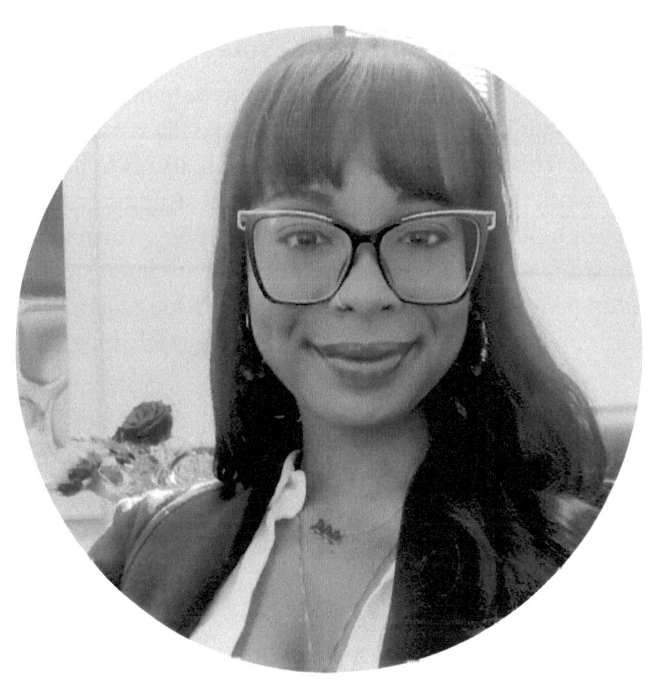

About the Author

Jamie Maxwell is a mother, survivor, writer, and certified substance use disorder counselor. A former foster youth, Jamie brings a unique blend of lived experience and professional wisdom to every piece she writes. Her words are a reflection of resilience forged in the fire of real-life hardships—addiction, displacement, recovery, and healing.

She is currently continuing her education with a focus on social justice and advocacy, aiming to open a nonprofit and transitional housing program to provide resources to her community, especially those impacted by mental health and substance use.

A proud single mother to her son, Sage, Jamie finds beauty in everyday survival. She writes for the women who never thought they'd make it, for the people labeled as "too broken," and for the souls who have decided to rise again—golden cracks and all.

Publisher's Note

Daxson publishing was created to help marginalized artists and their allies publish their work, so the world can hear their voice. The vision for this publishing house is to help people get their work out there, and not have them struggle finding their way through the publishing process. Everyone's voice deserves to be heard, and we are here to help. If you are interested in submitting a manuscript, email daxsonpublishing@gmail.com. Support our cause! Buy our books at daxsonpublishing.com.

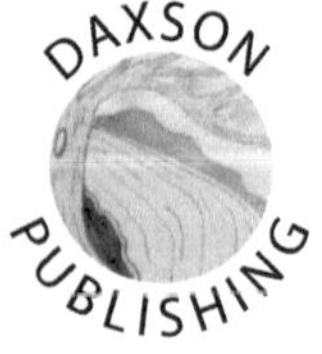

www.Ingramcontent.com/pod-product-compliance
Ingram Content Group UK Ltd.
Pitfield, Milton Keynes, MK11 3LW, UK
UKHW041846200726
13854UKWH00005BA/2269

9 781966 337263